T0097953

A Gift of Good Wishes

Karen Moore

Bristol Park Books

Bristol Park Books
252 West 38th Street
New York, NY 10018

Bristol Park Books is a registered trademark
of Bristol Park Books, Inc.

Library of Congress Control Number: 2016937085

ISBN: 978-0-88486-622-0

E-Book ISBN: 978-0-88486-623-7

Text and cover design by Keira McGuinness
Cover art copyright © 2016 Varvara Gorbash / Shutterstock

Printed in Malaysia

To

_____

From

_____

Introduction:

A Gift of Good Wishes communicates the kindness of your heart to your dearest friends or even those you have only known a short time. It helps you wish them all the very best that life can bring.

Good wishes are offered with friendship and love; from that place within that celebrates all that is meaningful in life. Granting wishes has long been the cornerstone of fairytale lore and has roots in ancient cultures. It's a hope that never subsides; a gift to hold forever. Good wishes given and received bring their own kind of joy.

So give your good wishes to your dearest friends, to the people you know who are getting married, to the person who just graduated from college and to the ones who've blessed your life in a multitude of ways.

It's your turn to be either the recipient of good wishes or the one who offers those beautiful thoughts to others.

May all your wishes come true!

—*Karen Moore*

Wishing on a Star

We probably all have our favorite "wishing places." One of my favorites is to look up at the twinkling night sky and wish upon a star. If wishing on a star would cause dreams to come true for people I love, I would never cease my star-gazing. I would always wish for the things I imagine would make you the happiest. Wishing is a form of hope and I hope for the best for you. I hope for the things that bring more promise to your life.

I wish for you to find fulfillment in your work and to be free to dream about tomorrow, trusting that more opportunities will reveal themselves to you each day. I wish for you to be fully satisfied with your choices and happy in all that you do.

Nothing could make me smile more than knowing you are doing well and that your life feels abundant. May your dreams come true and may the stars brightly shine on each day of your life. For now and always, may you hold as many good wishes close to your heart, as there are stars in the heavens above.

Dreams do come true, if we only wish hard enough.
You can have anything in life if you will sacrifice
everything else for it.

—James M. Barrie

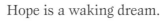

Hope is a waking dream.

—Aristotle

If seeds in the black earth can turn into such
    beautiful roses,
What might not the heart of man become
In its long journey toward the stars?

                     —*G. K. Chesterton*

Keep your eyes on the stars and your feet
    on the ground.

                     —*Theodore Roosevelt*

Starlight, star bright,
First star I see tonight.
I wish I may, I wish I might
Receive your gifts of love and light.

                     —*(adapted)*

The idea of wishing on a star dates back to the Romans who thought that the first star they could see at night was the one that was called the planet Venus. Since the Roman goddess for love was named Venus, it made sense to them to offer prayers to the goddess, hoping that she might answer their desires for love. Eventually, the prayers were simply made as wishes and the original meaning was changed. Over the years, it became more common to simply offer a wish to the first star you could see in the night sky. The hope of course, was that the goddess of love would answer.

Star-Gazing

The moonlit night

Is twinkling bright,

Cascading each white star.

And there is one

That's like the sun—

The biggest star by far.

It beckons quietly to me

To make a wish and stop and see

The light show it provides—for in its beams

Are endless dreams

Where happiness resides.

When You See a Wishing Star

When you see a wishing star
Beaming joy right where you are
It's your chance to receive
Your wishes, if you just believe—
Because you hold within your heart
The place where all good wishes stay.

Only the heart knows how to find what is precious.
—Fyodor Dostoevsky

A dream is a wish your heart makes.
—Walt Disney

I know nothing with any certainty, but the sight
of the stars makes me dream.
—Vincent Van Gogh

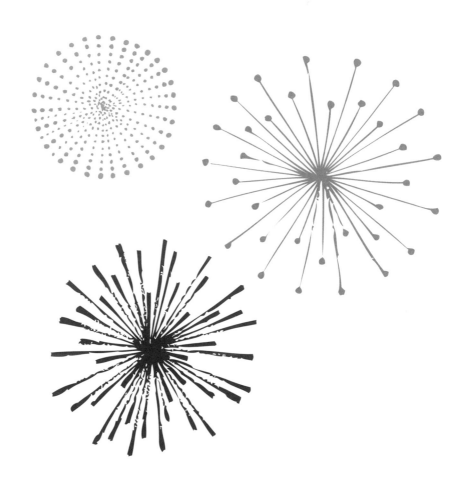

Every great dream begins with a dreamer. Always
remember, you have within you the strength,
the patience, and the passion to reach for the stars
to change the world.

—Harriet Tubman

Be glad of life because it gives you the chance to
love, to work, to play, and to look up at the stars.

—Henry Van Dyke

The heavens declare the glory of God;
And the firmament shows His handiwork.

—Psalm 19:1

Every heart sings a song, incomplete,
until another heart whispers back.
Those who wish to sing always find a song.

—Plato

We have the capacity to receive messages from the
stars and the songs of the night winds.

—Ruth St. Denis

Birthday Wishes

"Happy Birthday!" We celebrate that special day with a glowing

cake and a few friends and someone says, "Make a wish!" We close

our eyes, think of something we hope for, and then blow out the

lighted candles. Tradition suggests that if we blow them all out in

one breath we can expect our wishes to come true.

What did you wish for on your birthday? Whatever it was I hope

that your wish has come true by now. If it hasn't happened yet,

know that I'm standing with you, wishing with all my heart that

the things you hope for will happen in beautiful ways.

Whether you recently celebrated a birthday, or you have one coming soon, I wish you all the best things for a lifetime. May every birthday cause your light to shine brightly and may the wishes made on your birthday candles light up your face with a smile.

> Hope is the thing with feathers—
> That perches in the soul—
> And sings the tunes without the words—
> And never stops—at all.
>
> *—Emily Dickinson*

The Candles on Your Cake

If I could make a wish
On each candle on your cake,
I'd wish you great success
In every effort that you make.
I'd wish for laugh-filled days
And friends to sit a spell
As you all share favorite stories
That your hearts just long to tell.
I'd wish for peaceful moments
To reflect on where you've been
And for dreams to guide your steps
As you go on your way again.
I'd wish for love to hold you close
And hug you oh-so tight,
And I'd wish your life would overflow
With things that bring delight.
Yes, I'd wish on every candle,
You could never truly measure
The endless gifts life has for you,
With memories to treasure.

The practice of putting candles on a cake probably began with the ancient Greeks. They would make round cakes in honor of the goddess of the moon, Artemis. The lit candles reminded them of the moon's glow. When the candles were blown out, the smoke would then rise up to the gods and carry their wishes and prayers to the skies.

The more contemporary version of actually putting lighted candles on sweet cakes as a way to represent the "light of life" is attributed to the Germans. It has become tradition to bring a lighted cake for the birthday person to make a fond wish and then blow out the candles. Of course, the wish cannot be shared with anyone else, or it will not come true.

Birthday candles glow,
And joy is everywhere
Heartfelt wishes go.

There are two great days in a person's life;
the day we are born and the day we discover why.

—*William Barclay*

I think, at a child's birth, if a mother could ask a
fairy godmother to endow it with the most useful
gift, that gift should be curiosity.

—*Eleanor Roosevelt*

Hope lies in dreams, in imagination, and in
the courage of those who dare to make dreams
into reality.

—*Jonas Salk*

A Song in Your Heart

My wish for today
Is that your morning will start
With a smile on your face
And a song in your heart.

Then moving toward noon,
I hope you'll find your way
To a magical, marvelous,
Sun-shiny, warm day.

By the dinner time hour,
May you feel satisfied
That your day was enriched
By each thing that you tried.

With a song in your heart,
May the evening bring peace
And a sense of delight
That will just never cease.

We turn, not older with years, but newer every day.

—*Emily Dickinson*

Between the wish and the thing, life lies waiting.

—*Author unknown*

Look to this day…. In it lie all the realities
and verities of existence, the bliss of growth,
the splendor of action, the glory of power.
For yesterday is but a dream
and tomorrow is only a vision.
But today, well lived, makes every yesterday
a dream of happiness, and every tomorrow
a vision of hope.

—*Sanskrit proverb*

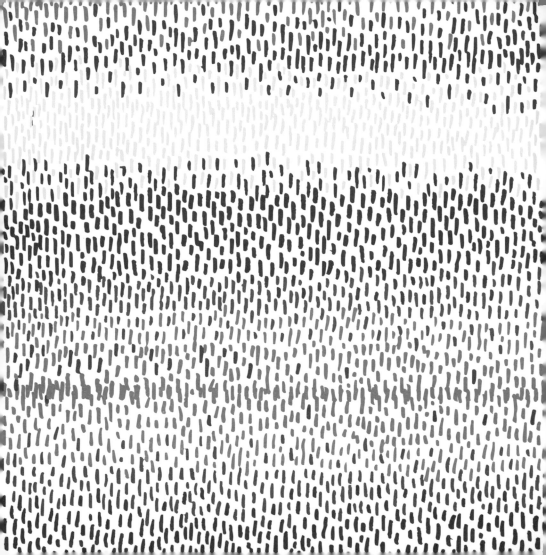

Rainbow Wishes

Rainbows are the beautiful symbols of hope and promise. They appear in the sky arrayed in their glory, effectively mixing the colorful sunshine and the blue-gray rain-filled sky. They remind us that life is sprinkled with benefits that filter down to us through sunshine and rain. When you see one of those amazing colorful arches stretching itself across the skies, it's a golden opportunity to make a few rainbow wishes.

If things are out of balance for you, I wish you clarity. I wish for the sun to shine on your troubles so that you can sense the promise of all that's ahead. I wish you a certainty that you are moving in the right direction and that those around you would support your path. I wish you a life full of wonder and colored by every imaginable joy.

When you can't find the gold at the rainbow's end, then I have another wish for you. I wish you the gift of quiet surrender, the chance to be confident as you simply hold on to the promise of all that is good. Trust that things will work out in your favor and that the needed balance of life will return. I wish you these things in sunshine and in rain.

> Will you not open your heart to know,
> What rainbows teach and sunsets show?
> —*Ralph Waldo Emerson*

A Rainbow Promise

If gold were at
The rainbow's end,
I'd wish for gold
For you, my friend.
I'd wish that you
Would be carefree
And win at life
Quite favorably.
I'd wish your heart
Would be at peace
And that all good things

Would never cease.
I'd wish each day
That you could view
A rainbow promise
For all you do.
I'd hope you'd find
The truest gold
Comes from the friendships
That you hold.
And I'd wish you days
That are displayed
With rainbow promises
Gently made…all for You!

May the road rise up to meet you.
May the wind be always at your back.
May the sun shine warm upon your face.
And may the rains fall softly upon your fields.
Until we meet again,
May God hold you in the hollow of his hand.

—Traditional Gaelic Blessing

Those who keep speaking about the sun
while walking under a cloudy sky
are messengers of hope.

—Henri J. Nouwen

Before the rain stops, we hear a bird.
Even under the heavy snows we see snowdrops.

—Shunryu Suzuki

Consult not your fears
But your hopes and your dreams.
Think not about your frustrations,
But about your potential.
Concern yourself not with what you tried
And failed in,
But with what it is still possible
For you to do.

—Pope John XXIII

The ninety and nine
Are with dreams, content
But the hope of the world made new,
Is the hundredth man
Who is grimly bent
On making those dreams come true.

—Edgar Allan Poe

My heart leaps up when I behold
A rainbow in the sky.

—*William Wordsworth*

The Colors of the Rainbow

The colors of the rainbow
From red to violet
Shimmer cross the open sky
Until each wish is set.
Each color of the rainbow
Stands for love and sweet success,
Sprinkled with our hopes for peace
And heartfelt happiness.
So when you see the rainbow
Make its way across the sky,
Then make a wish for those you love
As you are passing by.

Fountains of Wishes

There are many fountains around the world, but probably one of the best known is the Trevi Fountain in Rome. It was originally the endpoint of an aqueduct and named after the goddess, Virgo. It was thought that soldiers who were thirsty and tired could find drinking water and rest. Drinking from the fountain could bring good health and long life.

Today the Trevi Fountain is the place where imagination soars. The idea is that if you throw two coins in the fountain, you'll fall in love with a Roman. If you throw three coins into the fountain, you'll get married to that person. Hopeful hearts and endless tourists have been drawn to the site from around the globe

If I could be near that fountain today, I'd make wishes for you for the incredible gifts life has to offer. My wishes would go way

beyond those of romance, for I would make wishes for the love

of friends and family, and the love of doing your favorite things;

of experiencing simple pleasures that help you strive to achieve

your dreams. I imagine that I am throwing a coin into the beautiful

fountain where hope resides and good wishes find

new opportunities.

A Fountain of Wishes

If three coins could stand
  for wishes
In the fountain on the square,
I'd toss one in for happiness
Where nothing could compare.

I'd imagine all the special things
That fill your life with pleasure,
And wish you'd have more joy
Than you could ever measure.

I'd toss a coin for all the love
Your heart could ever hold
And ask that you would be
  embraced
By people, young and old.

The third coin would be better
Than the other two combined,
A coin that brings contentment
And endless peace of mind.

Yes, three coins in the fountain
Filled with wisdom, grace, and
  peace
And wishes that you'd always
  have
The joys that never cease.

In the case of fountains and wells, people toss in a
  coin while sending up a prayer—an early version
  of making a wish.

—Author unknown

There is hope in dreams, imagination, and in the
  courage of those who wish to make those dreams
  a reality.

—Jonas Salk

When you love someone all your saved up wishes
  start coming out.

—Elizabeth Bowen

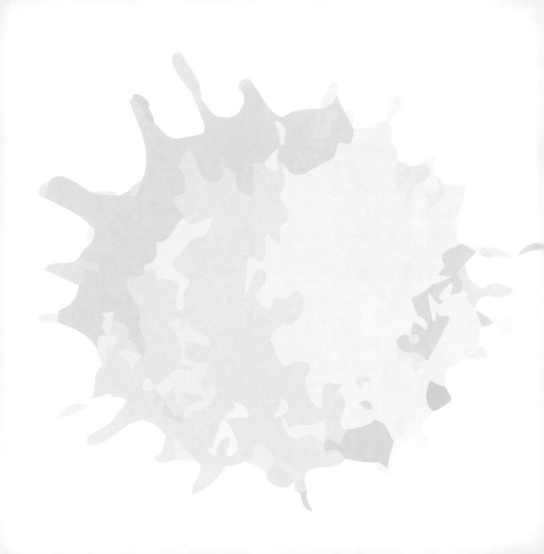

A Splash of Good Wishes

A splash for sweet surprises,
And beautiful sunrises,
Come rushing up with every water spray.

A splash for love and laughter
And friends forever after
Are the wishes in my heart for you today.

Yes, the fountains overflowing
Are the things that keep you going
And the ones that give you reasons yet to smile.

For a fountain spouts its glory
As it strives to share the story
That this precious gift of life is so worthwhile.

Make a Wish at The Fountain

Some go to the fountain
With its dancing water spray
And stand around for hours
Not knowing what to say.

They have a wish within them
That they'd like to make come true,
But when the moment comes along
They aren't sure what to do.

Should they toss a coin into the mist
And hope its magic brings
The dreams they've had for years
For a life of all good things?

They ponder and they wonder,
What will the fountain share?
Will it sprinkle them with wishes
And dreams beyond compare?

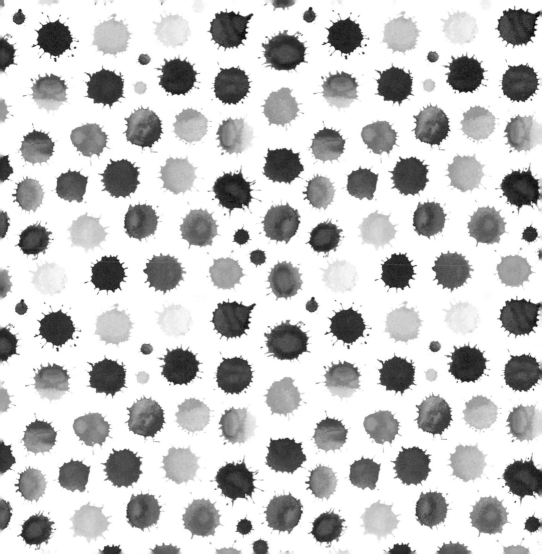

Alas, they'll never know
For they simply walk away
While the deepest wish within their hearts
Waits for another day.

So, if you go to the fountain
And you have a coin to toss,
Just heave it in and take your chance
On the win or on the loss.

> A kind heart is a fountain of gladness, making
> everything in its vicinity freshen into smiles.
> —*Washington Irving*

> Look within. Within is the fountain of good, and it
> will ever bubble up, if thou wilt ever dig.
> —*Marcus Aurelius*

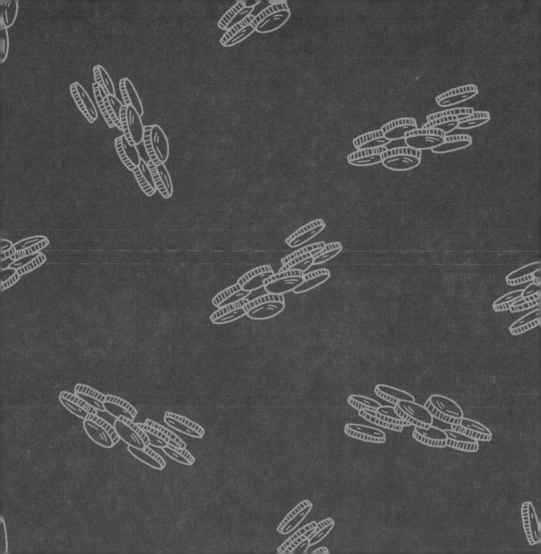

Moonlight Wishes

Standing beneath the glow of a beautiful moonlit sky, I send up wishes in your honor. I whisper my hopes for your well-being, for you to be healthy and strong, and for all good things to come your way. As I watch the moon, knowing that wherever you are, you can see the same moon, I'm filled with joy.

I wish for strength; the kind of strength that moves you along with wisdom and confidence. I wish for your success in the ways that mean the most to you, and for the opportunity for you to live life with gratitude and kindness.

Moonlight wishes are those that reflect the deepest desires of the heart. They are born through the powerful connection between friends and between those who share love for each other. May beautiful moonlight wishes find their way to you no matter where you may be today.

Where there is great love, there are always wishes.
—Willa Cather

To all, to each, A fair good-night,
And pleasing dreams, And slumbers light.
—Sir Walter Scott

Just Beneath the Moonlight

I tiptoed 'neath the moonlight
And was trapped within its glow
And I thought about the ones I love,
The ones I'm glad to know.

I started making wishes
That I hoped would bring delight
And shared them with the moon
On that quiet sparkling night.

I wished for health and happiness
And triumph over fear
And I wished that love would wipe away
Every kind of tear.

I wished for pleasant moments
To be enjoyed with special friends
And I wished for sweet contentment
That simply never ends.
I wished for all the best things
That my heart could think to say
And I wished that endless blessings
Would always come your way.

Yes, I tiptoed through the moonlight
And while I lingered there,
I wished for all your hopes and joys
Every day and everywhere.

Wish on the Moon on Your Birthday

You can make a wish on the moon on your birthday evening. If there is a crescent with its tips pointing up, then it means the moon may not grant your wish. If the tips of the crescent point down, your wish will come true. If there is a full moon on your birthday, then it means you will have a year of good luck.

Conversation with the Moon

I see the moon
Just past the hill
And it seems bright
But very still.

I search to find
Its mirrored face
As it shines down
In blissful grace.

I see the moon
And it sees me
And we each enjoy
Our company.

I wonder if
The moon and I
Share wishes
For each passer-by.

Yes, mystery
Wraps in the light
Of the silvery moon
On a starry night.

Dance with the Moon

I offered the moon my arm
   And we danced over the shimmering hills
  And moon-soaked fields.
We sprinkled stardust
  Over the meadows
  And offered our fondest wishes
  To those who help make our world go round.
It was a night for dancing
  And we were a star-struck pair,
  Reflecting joy
  And sending beams of love
  To everyone we knew.

      Shoot for the moon
      Wherever you are,
      If you miss the moon,
      You may land on a star.

Wishbone Wishes

As kids we wanted to be one of the two people that could break the dried out wishbone from the Thanksgiving turkey. We wished for something special to happen.

I can't remember if any of those wishbone wishes ever came true, but I know that it will always make sense to me to wish for the best things in life. If I could get that wishbone from the turkey now, here are some of the things I'd be wishing.

I'd wish that you would always have enough of everything; enough food, enough money, enough friends, enough hugs in a day, and whatever else gives you a sense of well-being. I'd wish for you to know that you are always loved and always valuable. I'd wish for you to be safe in your travels, content at home, and happy wherever you are.

Sometimes it's a good idea to make good wishes for yourself. You can wish for the best things:

> I wish to be content.
>
> I wish to be happy wherever I am.
>
> I wish to healthy and strong.
>
> I wish to be loving and kind.
>
> I wish every person felt loved.

Imagine yourself repeating those wishes until you believed them, trusted them, and acted as though they were true. It could change your whole day or even your life!

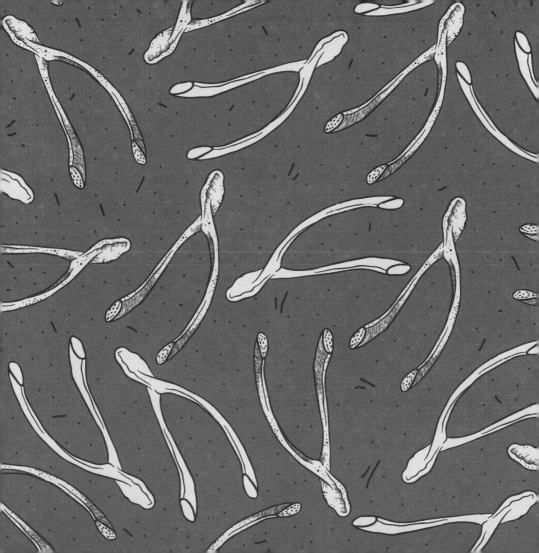

However many blessings we expect from God,
  His infinite liberality will always exceed all our
  wishes and our thoughts.

—John Calvin

We all have our own life to pursue,
Our own kind of dream to be weaving,
And we all have the power to make wishes come true
As long as we keep believing.

—Louisa May Alcott

Destiny grants us our wishes, but in its own way, in
  order to give us something beyond our wishes.

—Johann Wolfgang von Goethe

Breaking wishbones dates back to the Etruscans, an ancient Italian civilization. They believed chickens had prophetic powers. Chickens were placed in the middle of a circle divided into wedges to allow for each letter in the alphabet. Bits of food were scattered on each section, and scribes would take note of each wedge where the chickens snacked. The information the scribes received from the places where the chickens ate the food, was then taken to the local priests. The priests would use the chicken scratches to answer the city's questions about the future.

After the oracle chickens were killed, the wishbone was laid out in the sun to be preserved. People would rub and wish on the bone, believing it had the powers of the living chicken.

The Romans picked up this tradition and gave it their own twist. Two protect the small number of available wishbones, they determined that two people would share one wishbone and break it in half. The owner of the larger half was granted a wish.

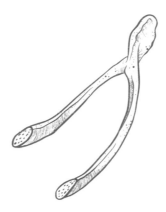

Don't Break the Wishbone!

The turkey is done,
Cooling off in the dish,
And when it is carved
We'll make a big wish.

We'll each grab an end
Of that delicate bone
And make a true wish
Of our very own.

We'll hold on real tight
And when we are ready,
We'll think of our wish
And keep the bone steady.

Then quick as a wink
We'll pull with our might
And hope for our wish
With our eyes closed up tight.

Then we'll hear the bone crackle
And snap right in two
And we'll see if our wishes
We'll really come true.

Whoever holds fast
To the biggest part
Will get the wish
They made with their heart.

So don't break the wishbone
'Til you're ready to see
If the wish to be granted
Is for you or for me!

Dandelion Wishes

Remember being a child, picking a dandelion, making a wish and blowing the fluffy seeds into the wind? It was fun to imagine that your wishes could come true as you watched the seeds go floating off in all directions.

I would enjoy making dandelion wishes for you. As seeds go gently spinning through the air, I would wish that each one would land on a place where new opportunity would grow just for you. Some seeds could fall upon the work you want to accomplish. Some would be drawn into the beautiful ideas you want to develop and the new goals you hope to achieve. Think of me gently blowing on a generous dandelion, ready to spread its wings and help you fly. It's a gift of scattered joy.

Apparently, the idea of wishing on a dandelion seed goes back to the ancient Celts and to the French. The actual word, "dandelion" comes from a French flower, *dent de lion*, which means "lion's tooth." Dandelions were used for medicinal purposes and so it was thought that you might wish on the seeds and they would bring healing.

In matters of love it was said that if you could blow all the seeds off a dandelion in one blow than you would be blessed by a passionate love. If seeds remained on the dandelion, then you may not be as loved as you had hoped.

Dandelion Wishes

I blew on a dandelion
That had just gone to seed,
And I made some special wishes
On that fluffy little weed.

I held the stem so closely
As I whispered my request
Then watched the seeds go dancing
From the East, out to the West.

I asked that every seed
That had taken to the air
Would make a wish come true for you—
Each place and everywhere.

I wished for love and gladness
And things that make you smile,
And I wished for loving memories
That make your life worthwhile.

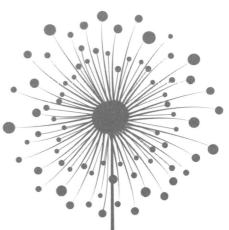

I wished you'd find the beauty
In every moment of a day
And that you'd keep on trying
When things don't go your way.

I wished for lots of laughter
For you to share with friends
And I wished that you'd have joy
That simply never ends.

I wished upon a dandelion
And puffed with all my might
And every tiny seed
Went twirling toward the light.

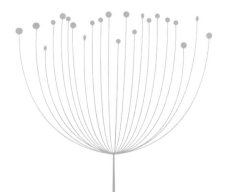

I knew then that the wishes
Would certainly come true
Because I wished with all my heart
The nicest things for you!

A Dandelion Story

Once upon a time,
A woman in great need
Chanced upon a dandelion
Lately gone to seed.

She plucked it from the soil
And held it to the sky
And blew the feathered weed
With a weary, hope-filled sigh.

She watched the seeds go dancing
Across the meadow land
As she let the load she carried
Fall gently from her hand.

It was a simple gesture,
But it cleared her worried mind
And caused her to imagine
Good things she might yet find.

As the woman went her way again
She smiled with delight
For her heart was filled with hope
Things would all work out just right.

The longest day comes to a close—
Gloomy nights fade with the dawn.
As our cares are washed away
We find the strength to carry on.

> The natural flights of the human mind are not from
> pleasure to pleasure, but from hope to hope.
> —*Samuel Johnson*

Daisy Petal Wishes

Pick a daisy! You may remember a grade school crush that caused you to pick a daisy, pull hopefully on each tender petal and wish that the person you liked, would like you right back. It appears that our Norse ancestors symbolized the goddess of love with a daisy. Hard to imagine the mighty warriors of ancient times pulling daisy petals, but love has always been a powerful force to be reckoned with. Because daisies are simple unassuming flowers, they were thought to symbolize the virtues of purity and innocence and love.

If I could make wishes for you , I'd make one new wish for each petal of the daisy, trusting that the intentions of my heart could be heard and honored. These would be the wishes that remain childlike, the ones for perpetual youth and a refreshing spirit.

I might wish that the dreams of your youth might come to fruition now. I would wish that your heart would remain light and free and willing to try again when you fall down, willing to seek a new moment in the sun.

Picking Daisies

I was walking in the countryside,
One briskly bright spring day
When I saw a field of daisies
Lift their heads and start to play.

They beckoned me to come along
Instead of passing through,
So I walked among the flowers
And made wishes just for you.

One petal danced with happiness
As it reached out for the sun
And granted wishes for success
In the work that you've begun.

Another simply shared with me
That wishes often blend
The thoughts and special dreams
That support each loving friend.

I wished for opportunities
To make your spirit dance
And I wished for things that give you room
To take another chance.

I wished for little worries
That might hold you back a bit
To simply step aside
For your joy and benefit.

As the petals started falling
So gently to the ground,
Wishes echoed 'cross the field
And made the sweetest sound.

I was grateful for the moments
That the daisies offered me
And the field was filled with smiles
As far as I could see.

Just living is not enough…one must have sunshine,
Freedom, and a little flower.

—*Hans Christian Andersen*

How does the meadow flower its bloom unfold?
Because the lovely little flower
Is free down to its root,
And in that freedom bold!

—*William Wordsworth*

Nobody sees a flower really; it is so small. We
haven't time, and to see takes time — like to have
a friend takes time.

—Georgia O'Keeffe

Wishing Wells

For centuries, those seeking a blessing or an answer to their hopes
and dreams would toss a coin into a well. They hoped the spirits
of the well would favor them with their request. It all started in
ancient Celtic and Norse traditions because finding a fresh water
spring where a well could be placed, appeared to be a special sign
of favor. Interestingly, the tradition lingers on and people the world
over still toss coins into the wells of fortune, hoping that they too
will receive good wishes.

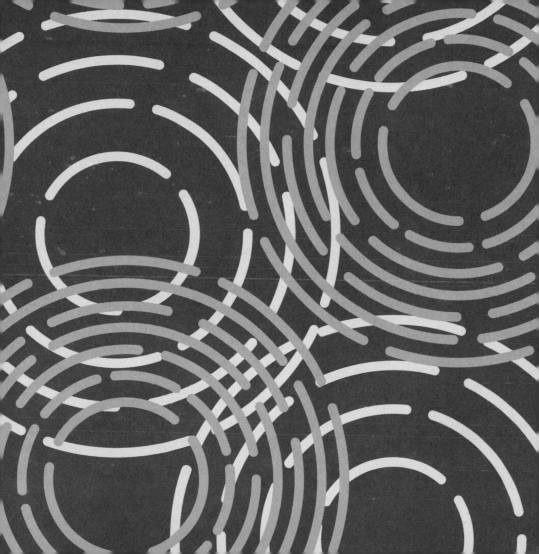

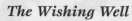

The Wishing Well

I went to the wishing well
With lots of things to say,
Just seeking special favor
For all that comes your way.

I dropped a coin and waited
To hear it hit the ground
And after several moments
I heard a tinkling sound.

And so I spoke quite clearly,
Those wishes of the heart
That I hoped would find an answer
To give you a brand new start.

I hoped the well's clean waters
And its quiet natural spring
Would somehow take my wishes
And make your spirit sing.

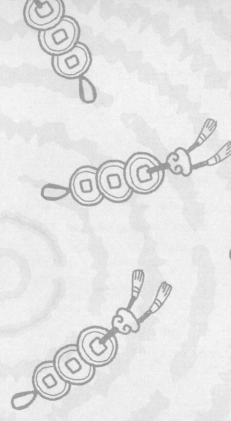

But, perhaps there's no real magic
In a well from days gone by,
But I believe in all good wishes
So the well was worth a try.

One thing I know for certain
Is that wishes from the heart
Are always a good place for joy
To find a brand new start.

And so I found a wishing well
And wished with all my might
For things to make you smile
And fill you with delight!

We have within ourselves enough to fill the present
   day with joy,
And overspread the future years with hope.
                 —*William Wordsworth*

Never part with your illusions. Without dreams you
may continue to exist, but you have ceased to live.
                 —*Mark Twain*

Shooting Stars

You may not be able to "catch a falling star" as one song suggests, but you can look up at the heavens with the same awe that our ancestors did, and enjoy the beauty of a shooting star. Of course, these shooting stars are not really stars at all, but meteorites putting on one last light show.

We've wished on shooting stars since the days of Ptolemy, and we still find them intriguing. Perhaps that's why I think shooting stars are good reasons for sending up wishes for the people we love. I've always been drawn to the *Starry Night* painting of Van Gogh. Maybe it's because there could be numerous shooting stars there, swirling through the skies, bringing the gift of good wishes to those below.

Look up! There may just be a shooting star with a gift of good wishes for you.

It seems to me we can never give up longing and wishing while we are thoroughly alive. There are certain things we feel to be beautiful and good, and we must hunger after them.

—*George Eliot*

Shooting Stars and Wishes

There's nothing like a starry night
To bring sparkle to your eyes,
And if you see a shooting star
Your joy just multiplies.

It brings a chance for wishes
To be whispered then and there
And as they're sent up to the heavens
They're almost like a prayer.

You can wish for something special,
Something that you feel,
Deep within your heart
That is too tender to reveal.

You can wish for joy for others,
And lift your spirits high
As you watch that shooting star
Go streaking 'cross the sky.

Yes, there's nothing like a starry night,
When stars just brightly shine
And illuminate the hopes and dreams
Of hearts like yours and mine.

There are two kinds of light…
The glow that illuminates,
And the glare that obscures.

—*James Thurber*

Reach high, for stars lie hidden in your soul.
Dream deep, for every dream precedes the goal.
                    —*Pamela Starr (1909)*

Penny Wishes

"Find a penny, pick it up and all day long you'll have good luck. Give a penny to a friend, and then your luck will never end."

You probably remember that old saying about finding a penny. That may well be so, especially if we add to it the Benjamin Franklin adage that "a penny saved is a penny earned." It's also said that if you toss a penny over your left shoulder, and make a wish your wish will come true.

Remember penny loafers? Those shoes somehow meant that we would carry our good luck with us all through the day. So, here's a penny for your thoughts and a chance to wish for all the good things life has to offer.

Pennies are unique because they have little value as one simple coin, but great value as they grow. Wishes are like that. One wish alone may not make your dreams come true, but as you focus on your choices, your direction, and your intentions in life, you'll see opportunities that didn't appear before, and you'll discover ways for your dreams to become clearly possible.

So put a penny in your shoe and a smile on your face and make today a masterpiece.

My Penny Wishes for You

Today I found a penny
As I walked down the street
And I stopped to pick it up
And made a wish for something sweet.

I wished for friends like you
To have a perfect day
And I wished for happiness
In your work and in your play.

I wished for gifts of joy
In the workings of your hands
And that you'd find fulfillment
In all your dreams and plans.

I wished that you'd be healthy,
Carefree, wise, and strong
And that you'd always have a sense
Of the places you belong.

I wished for quiet moments
To reflect on all you do
And that every choice you make
Would be wise and sure and true.

I wished for lots of laughter
As you gather with your friends
And I wished for love's abundance
That never breaks, but always bends.

I wished for all good things
Because each time I do,
I know those special wishes
Are the ones you'd wish me too.

Do not seek to bring things to pass in accordance
    with your wishes,
But wish for them, as they are, and you will find
    them.

—Epictetus

A Gift of Good Wishes

This little book of wishes
Was made for you, my Friend,
To remind you that you're always wished
The joys that never end.

So, whether you wish on a star,
Blow out candles on a cake,
Or toss coins into a fountain
To receive each wish you make,

Or if you spot a rainbow
And makes wishes to the sky
Or wish on shooting stars
As they go passing by,

You're wished the greatest joys
That life can send your way
With the gift of these good wishes
Meant for every single day.

Illustration Credits